Charles Haddon
Spurgeon

June 19, 1⟨...⟩ 31, 1892

WOMEN OF FAITH SERIES

Amy Carmichael
Corrie ten Boom
Florence Nightingale
Gladys Aylward
Hannah Whitall Smith
Isobel Kuhn
Mary Slessor

MEN OF FAITH SERIES

Borden of Yale
Brother Andrew
C. S. Lewis
Charles Finney
Charles Spurgeon
Eric Liddell
George Muller
Hudson Taylor
Jim Elliot
Jonathan Goforth
John Hyde
John Wesley
Martin Luther
Samuel Morris
Terry Waite
William Carey

John and Betty Stam

MEN OF FAITH

Charles Spurgeon

Kathy Triggs

BETHANY HOUSE PUBLISHERS
MINNEAPOLIS, MINNESOTA 55438
A Division of Bethany Fellowship, Inc.

Originally published in England in 1984 as *Charles Spurgeon: The Boy Preacher of the Fens* by Pickering & Inglis.

Charles Spurgeon
Kathy Triggs

Library of Congress Catalog Card Number 86-70909

ISBN 0-87123-667-2

Published by Bethany House Publishers
A Division of Bethany Fellowship, Inc.
6820 Auto Club Road, Minneapolis, Minnesota 55438

Printed in the United States of America

Contents

1   The Boy Preacher
of the Fens
(1834 – 1853)

There is an old saying, *'The heart makes the theologian,'* and Charles Haddon Spurgeon's theology certainly came from his heart. He was convinced of God's love for him, and of God's desire to save all who would come to him. This was Spurgeon's great message throughout his life. And it may be that his heart was all the more ready to accept the love of God because he had been brought up in an atmosphere of love and affection. By Victorian standards he was even spoiled.

He was born in Kelvedon, Essex, on the nineteenth of June 1834, the eldest son of John and Eliza

Spurgeon. John was an Independent (Congregational) minister, serving a small church in Tollesbury, some ten miles away. As his congregation could not afford a sufficient salary he added to his income by working as an accountant for a Kelvedon coal merchant.

The first years of John and Eliza's marriage seem to have been beset with financial difficulties. When Charles was ten months old they moved to Colchester, and four months later the child was taken to live with his grandparents, perhaps because the Colchester house was unhealthy for him. James and Sarah Spurgeon, John's parents, lived in Stambourne, an Essex village midway between Halstead and Haverhill. James Spurgeon was minister of the Independent Chapel there, and was greatly loved by the whole village.

There was a strong tradition of religious dissent in the Spurgeon family. Several of Spurgeon's ancestors had been Independent ministers, and one individual, John Spurgeon, had fallen foul of the authorities in Charles the second's day, for attending Nonconformist meetings. He had been fined and, on a subsequent occasion, put into prison. It is thought that some of Spurgeon's ancestors were Dutch Protestant refugees, who fled to England from Roman Catholic persecution in 1568 and settled in Essex. As a man Charles Spurgeon had the round face and stocky body that is characteristic of the Netherlands.

Two formative elements in the young Spurgeon's life, therefore, were the strong Puritan tradition in his family (and this was exemplified in his grandfather's conduct and beliefs), and the loving care of his grand-parents and his aunt Ann. She was only seventeen when he went to stay, and delighted as much as her parents in the little boy who was to be mothered, loved and fussed over, petted and generally made much of. It was Ann who taught him to read; she also encouraged his sense of fun. Throughout his life he loved jokes and riddles, and even in his mature years was not above the odd practical joke.

There was no question of being seen and not heard with the little Charles. He was a bright little boy, and was always asking questions. He soon discovered that if he was not satisfied at once, gentle persistence would generally bring him the explanation he wanted. He would even interrupt the daily Bible reading if there was something in it he did not understand. He was never punished for these interruptions, but was met with patience and love. Under this régime his mental powers began to blossom, along with a dawning understanding of spiritual matters.

The manse at Stambourne was unusually large for a dissenting minister's house. In Charles' day many of its windows were boarded up so that the window-tax need not be paid on them. The house was for the little boy a treasury of cool, dark rooms to be explored, in which he might find all sorts of wonderful things, from old books to the best china. It was an old, tottery house, with so much space around the window frames that the rambling roses and the ivy used to grow through into the rooms. Swallows built their nests on the outside wall, and sparrows had found a hole and made *their* nest right inside the wall.

Stambourne was unusual for the period in that a true Christian spirit prevailed there. Charles' grandfather had an excellent relationship with the Anglican rector, a Mr Hopkins. The two were great friends, and even shared some members of their congregations. The Squire, for instance, went to Church on Sunday morning and to Chapel in the afternoon. Charles remembered going to the Squire's for tea, with Mr Hopkins and his grandfather. The little boy and the three old boys all had sugared bread and butter for a treat. Charles grew up with the assumption that Christians should be friends in spite of differences of denomination. When he was a man, although he was unsparing in his criticism of 'heresy', he retained a surprisingly open mind towards members of other denominations. He had an excellent relationship with Dr Benson, Archbishop of Canterbury. He studied and learned from the writings of great Christians, whatever their denominations; he particularly admired John Wesley, in spite of his being a Methodist and an opponent of Calvinism.

His grandfather was a Calvinist of the old school, believing that those chosen by God are saved through no merit of their own and are unable to do anything by themselves to please God; his saving power overcomes all resistance on the part of the soul, and ensures that in spite of all lapses it will never lose its faith – 'once saved, always saved'. The Atonement was limited to God's chosen ones, his 'elect'. Charles was to grow up adhering strongly to these tenets, which were popularly known as the 'Five Points of Calvinism'.

James Spurgeon's congregation were mainly country people; most of Stambourne came to the Sunday afternoon services – about six hundred souls. They were a sturdy folk who knew what they wanted from their preacher. Old Spurgeon was noted among them for his preaching. His plain and practical sermons suited them admirably. As the minister's grandson young Charles attended chapel regularly. He became quite used to sitting on a hassock in one of the big square pews ('holy loose-boxes') with a peppermint to suck. The towering pulpit had a huge sounding-board hung over it. The little boy used to watch and wonder what would happen if it dropped upon his grandfather. The old man might be squashed up inside the pulpit like his grandson's jack-in-the-box!

As well as attending Sunday services, young Charles also attended the Sunday School run by the Stambourne Independents. There he learned Isaac Watts' Catechism – *'so simple, so interesting, so suggestive, that a better condensation of Scripture knowledge could never be written.'* We can be confident that he asked questions, persisting until he understood what he was learning. If the teachers would not help, he could always ask his grandfather. Religious education was to him full of interest and pleasure. He never knew the painful, frustrating business of having to learn something that sounded gibberish.

He soon discovered the library of a former minister, still intact in a darkened study opening off one of the manse bedrooms. He first laid hold of a big folio of

Bunyan's *Pilgrim's Progress,* then Foxe's *Book of Martyrs.* The library contained many of the great puritan works of the seventeenth and early eighteenth centuries – Baxter's *Call to the Unconverted,* Scougal's *The Life of God in the Soul of Man* and Doddridge's *Rise and Progress of Religion in the Soul.* As a man he loved the old puritan books, and would buy any he could get hold of. At his death he left a magnificent library containing many first editions.

One important thing that young Spurgeon learned from his grandfather was to do always what he believed right, whatever the consequences. James Spurgeon must have been aware that Charles already had a stubborn streak in him; perhaps he did not realise how much his advice went to increase that stubbornness. When Charles returned to Colchester in 1840 he got into trouble over this very issue. The congregation at Stambourne had always repeated the last line of every hymn, and the six year-old Charles, believing it to be morally right, continued the practice in the Colchester chapel. It took a lot of persuasion, and even punishment, to convince him that in some cases it must be his parents who should judge what is right. But in later life he was always grateful to his grandfather for his emphasis on integrity of conscience.

Charles missed his grandparents and aunt at first, but his return to Colchester was not entirely unhappy. His grandfather had told him to look at the moon and remember that it was the same moon as he himself was looking at from Stambourne.

'And for years, as a child, I used to love the moon because I thought that my grandfather's eyes and my own somehow met there on the moon.'

Life in Colchester was very different from that in Stambourne. Charles found himself suddenly the oldest of four children; he had acquired a brother, James, and two sisters, Eliza and Emily (his mother had seventeen children altogether, nine of whom died in infancy). He became the natural leader of the games, whether making and sailing toy boats, or playing at preaching in the stable, with the hay-rick for pulpit and the manger for a pew. The family had moved to a house on Hythe Hill. It had a little garden where the children were allowed to plant seeds. Typically, it was Charles who wanted to see what the seeds looked like while they were growing.

Charles had begun his formal schooling at the 'Dame School' in Stambourne. At Colchester he went to a similar school. He always looked forward to the holidays, when he could go to stay at Stambourne. One summer his grandmother asked him to learn Dr Watts's hymns, promising a penny for each. But he learned them so easily and quickly that the old lady began to be out of pocket. She reduced the price to a halfpenny, then to a farthing each. She was saved from financial ruin by her husband's offering a shilling a dozen for all the rats Charles could kill. Charles found this occupation even more lucrative, but he never forgot the hymns he had learned.

When he was ten years old he had a remarkable encounter at Stambourne. Richard Knill, who had been a missionary in India and Russia, was touring Essex on behalf of the London Missionary Society. He stayed at Stambourne Parsonage, and soon made the acquaintance of young Charles, who was on holiday at the manse. At six o'clock in the morning he called for Charles and took him into the garden, where he talked about Jesus, and how good it was to love and trust him in childhood. He prayed for the boy, kneeling down with his arms about Charles' neck. He did this for three successive days, then, before he left Stambourne, he said in the presence of the whole family, *This child will one day preach the gospel, and he will preach it to great multitudes.'* He added that Charles would surely preach in Rowland Hill's chapel – the Surrey Chapel, London. He called upon all present to witness his words, and made Charles promise that when he preached in that chapel he would use Cowper's hymn, *'God moves in a mysterious way his wonders to perform.'* The grown-up Charles was to preach many times in the Surrey Chapel. He kept his promise and used Cowper's hymn on the first occasion.

The ten year-old boy could not but be impressed by Richard Knill's words, and he began to consider himself as a future minister. But his father and grandfather had taught him that one who was not a truly converted Christian should not dare to enter the ministry. He began to hope that one day in the future he would be converted – that he too would experience the person of Christ.

The same year he left the Dame School and went to Stockwell School in Colchester. It was a day school, and Spurgeon used to take a packed lunch. He often had a joke book with him, and over lunch he would try out the jokes and riddles on his friends. Many a time the boys would choke over their food as they tried to eat, read and laugh at the same time. Spurgeon was rather a plump boy, not physically strong. He was not good at running or throwing games, but maintained his popularity by his quick wit and sense of fun. It is probably at Stockwell School that he developed his delight in the ready response that characterised his adult years. As boy and man he was determined to have the last word. His intelligence showed in his school work; he quickly got himself to the top of the class and kept his place there. Only one winter did he lose his top position — that was because he decided he wanted to be at the bottom:

> *'My teacher could not understand my unusual stupidity, until it suddenly occurred to him that I had purposely worked my way from the head of the class, which was opposite a draughty door, down to the foot, which was next to the stove. He therefore reversed the position of the scholars, and it was not long before I had again climbed to place of honour, where I also had the enjoyment of the heat from the fire.'*

When he was fourteen, Spurgeon went for a year to a Church of England school in Maidstone. The attraction for his parents was that his uncle, Mr David Walker, was the Maths master there. Charles had a happy twelve months. He soon became so proficient in Mathematics as to be able to correct his uncle when he made a mistake in the problem he was working out on the blackboard. Mr Walker was greatly offended at being corrected before all his pupils, but Charles maintained that he would have been wrong not to point out the mistake once he had noticed it. Knowing his nephew's stubborness, and perhaps fearing further corrections in class, Mr Walker allowed Charles to take his books and study by himself under an oak tree beside the River Medway.

Charles also had skirmishes with the masters in Religious Education classes. There were three clergymen who took it in turns to teach the Prayer Book catechism; one of them in particular took up the young Spurgeon on the matter of baptism. Independents practised infant baptism, but in a rather half-hearted and even (let it be said) superstitious manner. The clergyman led Charles to see that faith and repentance are necessary for baptism, as the Prayer Book states. He hoped that Spurgeon would thereupon concede the Anglican position, which accepts the promise of sponsors as the equivalent of faith and repentance. He was disappointed to discover that Spurgeon was more likely to become a Baptist.

'I resolved, from that moment, that if ever Divine grace should work a change in me, I would be baptised, since, as I afterwards told my friend the

16

*clergyman, "I never ought to be blamed for
improper baptism, as I had nothing to do with it;
the error, if any, rested with my parents and grand-
parents." '*

Spurgeon had no doubts at all that, although he was
the son and the grandson of a minister, and had been
baptised as a baby, he was not a Christian. He could
not fail to be aware of it when his mother spent time,
prayers and tears in exhorting her children to turn to
the Lord. It was her usual practice on a Sunday evening, when her husband had set out for the service at
Tollesbury, to gather the children around her. They
read from the Bible verse by verse, and she expounded
it to them; then she would read a passage from
Alleyne's *Alarm to the Unconverted* or from Baxter's
Call to the Unconverted, interspersed with *'pointed
observations made to each of us as we sat round the
table.'* Mrs Spurgeon would ask how long it would be
before they began to think about their state before
God, before they began to seek him. Then she would
pray in such terms as to wring the heart and stir the
conscience of them all. She knew her eldest son's stubbornness, and would pray particularly for him.
Charles was not impervious to her prayers and pleadings; in fact, he had a very tender conscience, and
needed no-one to point out his wrongdoings as a child.
As often as not he would cry himself to sleep over
them. But he would not seek God's forgiveness. Again
and again he put off the moment, supposing that,
'When I had nothing else to do, I might think of him

whose blood could cleanse me.' And so the months rolled by.

But gradually his tender conscience began to play its part, and he was gripped by a sharp sense of his own sinfulness. He felt he was too wicked even to pray to God, that God could never forgive him. The devil seemed to be claiming him for his own, pouring wicked thoughts into his mind. His profane and blasphemous thoughts troubled him, but the worst time was when he first considered the notion that there might be no God, no Christ, no heaven and no hell. At first he liked the idea, but before long he was horrified at the images of evil that swarmed after it. He plunged as if mesmerised into the abyss of doubt, until he even began to doubt his own existence. Then,

> *'The very extravagance of doubt proved its absurdity, and there came a voice which said "And can this doubt be true?" Then I awoke from that death-dream . . .'*

The experience convinced Charles that he desperately needed salvation. He prayed, but as God seemed to turn a deaf ear he began to despair, and became almost suicidal. His mother comforted him; she had never known of anyone who had sought Christ and been rejected. Charles thought that he would try praying once more. He went and *'Threw himself on the mercy of God.'*

His prayer was soon to be answered, although he did not know it. He had been in a state of intermittent spiritual anxiety for roughly five years, which included his time at Stockwell School and at the College in Maidstone. Now, in August 1849, he went to Newmarket Academy, whose head and proprietor was a Mr John Swindell. It took about sixteen day boys and boarders. Here Spurgeon was employed as an 'usher', or articled pupil: he was to teach the younger boys while receiving some tuition himself. He became great friends with J. D. Everett the assistant master, who later became a Fellow of the Royal Society and a Professor at Queen's College, Belfast. Everett described Spurgeon thus:

> *'He was rather small and delicate, with pale but plump face, dark brown eyes and hair, and a bright, lively manner, with a never failing flow of conversation. He was rather deficient in muscle, did not care for cricket or other athletic games, and was timid at meeting cattle in the roads.*
>
> *. . . He knew a little Greek, enough Latin to gather the general sense of Virgil's* Aeneid *without a dictionary, and was fond of algebra . . . He was a smart, clever boy at all kinds of book learning; and, judging from the accounts he gave me of his experience in his father's counting-house, he was also a smart man of business. He was a keen observer of men and manners, and very shrewd in his judgments. He enjoyed a joke, but was earnest, hard-working, and strictly conscientious.'*

Spurgeon's first term at Newmarket ended when 'fever' broke out in the school. He returned to Colchester for a lengthy winter holiday, having escaped the infection himself. He resolved to attend all the different churches in Colchester, *'in order that I might find out the way of salvation.'* The various sermons he heard fell wide of the mark as far as he was concerned. He wanted to discover what he should do to be saved.

On Sunday the sixth of January 1850, he set out to walk into the centre of Colchester. However a snowstorm quickly made progress impossible, and he turned into Artillery Street, not far from Hythe Hill, where there was a Primitive Methodist Chapel. The snow prevented the minister from reaching the chapel, and one of the members of the congregation took his place in the pulpit. Spurgeon was not at first very impressed: *'At last a very thin-looking man, a shoemaker, or tailor, or something of that sort, went up into the pulpit to preach.'* The man was uneducated, and could do little more than repeat the words of his text, which was, *'Look unto me and be ye saved, all the ends of the earth.'* But seeing the young Spurgeon sitting under the gallery he addressed him directly: *'Young man, you look very miserable. And you always will be miserable − miserable in life and miserable in death − if you don't obey my text.'* In that instant Charles felt as if the darkness had rolled away and he saw the sun. He looked to Christ and felt himself saved. *'I could have leaped, I could have danced; there was no expression, however fanatical, which would have been out of keeping with the joy of my spirit at that hour.'*

A particular concern in Charles' search for salvation was his anxiety to be rid of sin for ever. Now he was converted he thought he would be sinless, but before a week had elapsed he was discovering that the old Charles Spurgeon was very much alive and kicking. In fact, his sense of sin and need for repentance seemed stronger after his conversion than before it. He had not then read the works of Calvin; when he did so in later years he found that the 'Prince of Commentators' had understood his experience. Calvin says that faith and assurance come both at once when God reveals himself to the soul; repentance follows when the soul attempts obedience and finds how hard it is.

Spurgeon wrote a detailed account of his early religious experience, which was very similar to that of other notable puritans. Oliver Cromwell suffered a period of doubt and depression before his conversion, and so did John Bunyan. Their doubt was evidence of God's Spirit working within them. Spurgeon, however, was unable to see doubt as an instrument in the hand of the Almighty. For him it was a sin. He thought he had fallen into temptation because he had stopped listening to the voice of Revelation and heeded his own reason. In future he would cling to the Word of God. In later life he had little sympathy for the many Christians in the nineteenth century who, following the dictates of reason, felt compelled to give up their faith. He never saw that in fact reason and faith go hand in hand. His 'revelation' of the absurdity of doubt could equally well be a working – and a vindication – of reason.

Spurgeon returned to Newmarket at the end of January. He was homesick at first, missing the new-found intimacy with his parents. But his faith in Christ, the cause of that intimacy, helped him over this difficulty, and he settled down to his work. He taught Mathematics, but still found ample time for his own studies. Mr Swindell, who was a Baptist, helped him academically and spiritually. He had 'good religious conversations' with his usher, for which Spurgeon was very grateful, and helped him with French and Greek. The only difficulty for Charles was that he had all the less time for reading his Bible.

He received much sound instruction from the cook at the school, a godly old woman with a taste for 'good strong Calvinistic doctrine'. She and Charles would study the Bible together and discuss the basic tenets of Calvinism. These discussions helped Charles far more, in his estimation, than the sermons he heard at the Independent Chapel he attended in Newmarket. He soon decided to seek membership of this chapel, and was 'admitted to fellowship' on the fourth of April. He also wished to take the unusual step (for an Independent) of being baptised, and wrote to ask his father's permission. His mother had no objection; neither did his grandfather, but his father had some reservations. Charles also had to find a Baptist minister who would be willing to baptise an Independent. He wrote to Mr W. Cantlow of Isleham, a village about eight miles from Newmarket on the River Lark, and found that he had a 'baptising season' arranged for the end of April. Charles could join the other candidates, if his father would allow him to. Mr Spurgeon was slow in giving his consent, and Charles eventually wrote to his mother asking her to tell him how things stood. He was anxious to be baptised as soon as possible so that he could take communion:

> 'With my present convictions, I hope I shall never so violate my conscience as to (take communion) unbaptised . . . I assured the members at the church meeting that I would never do so.'

Meanwhile he was beginning to work in a small way as an evangelist. Mr Swindell encouraged the distribution of tracts, and Charles took over the thirty-three houses that had been on the round of his predecessor in the school. He found this very easy work; the conversations he had with his 'tract people' were a source of interest and encouragement to him. He longed to be, like his father, a successful preacher of the gospel.

The long awaited letter from his father came on the twenty-fifth of April. Mr Spurgeon gave his consent, but in such language as to make Charles feel he was badly used. After all, he was only following his conscience! On the twenty-sixth of April he noted in his diary,

> 'How my father's fears lest I should trust to baptism stir up my soul! My God, thou knowest that I hate such a thought! No, I know that, could I from this day be as holy as God himself, yet I could not atone for past sin.
> I have had a pretty good day. Fear, Mistrust and Timorous are yet at sword's length. May I be

Valiant-for-Truth, and live and die in my Master's glorious war!

On Friday the third of May 1850 – his mother's thirty-fifth birthday – Charles Spurgeon rose early for a couple of hours' quiet prayer before setting off to walk to Isleham. Mr Swindell had given him the day's holiday. From Isleham he walked with Mr Cantlow to Isleham Ferry, the spot on the River Lark which had been used for baptisms by five Baptist churches since 1798. There was a service held on the bank, followed by the baptism. Two women entered the water with the minister, then it was Charles' turn. On the bank he had been feeling cold and scared; in the water he felt only great joy. His 'timidity was washed away' and his tongue was loosened. He always afterwards had confidence in speaking of Christ to other people.

The following Sunday Spurgeon took his first Communion – 'A royal feast for me' – and taught in the Sunday School for the first time. He liked the Sunday School work and soon, as well as teaching a class, he was giving the short address at the close. Older people began to come when it was Charles' turn to speak, until the place looked like a chapel rather than a Sunday School.

In August Charles moved to a new school, in Cambridge. It was run by a Mr Leeding, who had first become known to the Spurgeons when he was an usher at Stockwell School in Colchester. Mr and Mrs Spurgeon must have been impressed by this young man's ability, for they kept in touch with him when he left Colchester to set up his own school in Union Road, Cambridge. Now John Spurgeon wrote to Mr Leeding, offering Charles' services free of charge in exchange for Mr Leeding's tuition. The Spurgeon family would pay for Charles' keep. This was a most welcome offer for Mr Leeding. He had often wished he had Charles' assistance, but could not afford to offer him the salary he felt his capabilities deserved. Now his difficulties were solved, and Charles was more than glad to go to a school run by such a good friend and teacher as Mr Leeding. The atmosphere of the school was one of pious studying. At eight o'clock every morning every person in the house went to their room for half an hour's prayer and meditation. When Charles was not teaching in the school he was studying theology – he was well past Greek and Latin exercises by now. Mr Leeding held the opinion that the sixteen year-old student could do well if he entered at Cambridge University. As a Dissenter Charles could have matriculated at Cambridge, but would not have been allowed to take his degree. But he was not interested in academic studies. He wanted to be a minister, and while a university course might be of use to Anglican clergymen, he suspected that it would be a drawback in Nonconformist circles. Nonetheless Spurgeon respected Cambridge University for its historical connections with Puritanism. Emmanuel College had been in many respects the seed-bed of the English Reformation, and no doubt even in 1850 many of the works of its most eminent divines were still available in the Cambridge bookshops.

When he moved to Mr Leeding's school Charles decided to leave the Independents and join the Baptist denomination. There were three Baptist chapels in Cambridge; Spurgeon went to St Andrew's Street Chapel, where he was soon involved in Sunday School work. On his first visit to the chapel nobody seemed ready to greet him, but after the communion service he addressed the man sharing his pew. This man was at first inclined to take a dim view of being accosted by an unknown sixteen year-old. Spurgeon persisted, saying that they were brothers, for *'When I took the bread and wine just now, in token of our being one in Christ, I meant it, did not you?'* The older man was struck by the lad's assumption that Christian fellowship was no fiction, and invited him to his home. So Charles' boldness and simplicity began to win him friends.

Old Mr Vinter of St Andrew's Street Chapel was in charge of the Cambridge Preachers' Association. Under his auspices young men would go out to preach the gospel in the villages surrounding the city. Vinter took a part in the preaching as well as helping and encouraging his young men, and he was always on the lookout for new talent. So it was that his eye fell upon the young Spurgeon. Guessing that a request to go and preach would be refused, he resorted to stratagem. One Saturday, at the close of morning school, Vinter called to ask Charles if he would go over to Teversham the following evening, *'For a young man was to preach there who was not much used to services, and very likely would be glad of company.'* Little did

Charles realise that the young man Vinter had in mind was himself! It was only in conversation with his companion on the road to Teversham that the truth came out. It appeared that if Charles did not preach, no-one would. Charles was, after all, quite used to giving talks in the Sunday School. So he preached his first sermon in a thatched cottage, to a handful of farm-labourers and their wives. He preached on the text, *'Unto you therefore which believe he is precious'*, but could not in later years remember what he actually said – only that he found it easier than he'd expected, and that he was delighted he'd not broken down in the middle of the service. His little congregation was amazed at his youthfulness; their congratulations gave him courage to continue in this spare-time work. Before long he was spending every evening walking to one or other of the thirteen villages in the district. He found the walking invaluable to him, for it gave him a period of quiet during which he could meditate on the theology he had been studying during the day, and prepare his mind for the simple talk that he was to give to the villagers. Preaching, he found, also helped him to fix the various aspects of the truth of the Gospel in his own mind. As well as the week-night preaching he was fully occupied on Sundays, with church services and Sunday School work. He would usually be invited to a friend's house for his meals. He wrote to his father, *'I have been busily employed every Lord's day; not at home once yet, nor do I expect to be this year.'*

In the autumn of 1851 Spurgeon was invited to be the pastor of the little Baptist chapel in Waterbeach, one of the villages in his district. The thatched building had once been a dovecote; it held forty members, who were too poor to pay a full-time minister's salary. Charles came to an arrangement with them by which he would continue to work as an usher, but would also spend his Sundays in Waterbeach, preaching morning, afternoon and evening. He would also preach there one evening in the week. For this he would receive forty-five pounds a year.

Spurgeon's first appearance at Waterbeach was inauspicious, as far as the deacons were concerned. He looked so young and pale that at least one of them thought to himself, 'He'll never be able to preach.' But when he got up to read the Bible, and began to explain the passage as he went along, the congregation realised that here was a preacher indeed. A full-length sermon followed, in which Spurgeon dealt with the topics of Justification and Sanctification. It is a mark of his ability that he was able to make such a difficult subject comprehensible to his rustic congregation.

He changed Waterbeach. The village had been notorious for drunkenness and its attendant evils of poverty, debauchery and violence. Soon the chapel was crowded and lives were reformed. Drunkenness became a thing of the past. Waterbeach had its effect on Spurgeon too. He made many blunders in his inexperience, but the villagers loved him, and there were always one or two wise old souls to put him right. Pomposity and self-conceit did not last long with them! He met not a few odd characters, and learned by experience how to deal with difficult cases. He was a little exasperated at first to find that many of 'his' villagers seemed to think that religion was a matter for the educated. He soon showed them that a man can be illiterate, yet full of wisdom in spiritual matters.

Then there were the Antinomians and the 'perfectionists' to deal with. The former were those who thought that once they were converted they had a licence to sin as they pleased, for Christ's death covered all their sins, past, present and future. Spurgeon warned them that as Christians their behaviour must be above reproach, or they would be despised even by unbelievers. They had an example in their own village which should make them pause for thought: a 'convert' was boasting of his salvation while drinking with his cronies in the local pub. The landlady had him thrown out of the window as a hypocrite. Spurgeon's method with those who believed they were perfect was to tease them a little. They invariably became angry, whereupon Spurgeon would point out that they were not so perfect as they had supposed.

Spurgeon's friends and spiritual advisers began to think that he would benefit from a course at a theological college. There was a Baptist College at Stepney, and in February 1852 its principal, Dr J. Angus, came to preach at Cambridge. Spurgeon was mentioned to him as a promising young minister, and a meeting was arranged. This was without Spurgeon's knowledge, so he was quite surprised to be asked to go and see Dr Angus at the house where he was staying. He went along at the appropriate time and was shown into the drawing-room. He waited nervously for a very long time, but nobody came. Eventually he had to return to his duties as an usher, so rang the bell. It turned out that Dr Angus had been waiting for him in the parlour, but had had to leave for London. The maid had told nobody of the young man waiting in the drawing-room! His opportunity was not lost, however, for Dr Angus left a kind note inviting him to apply to the College for the following September. The mistake meant that Spurgeon had time to think more carefully about the matter. His friends were all for the idea, but he was not so sure that they were right. He knew that his congregation at Waterbeach would miss him very much. In any case he was not too impressed with the type of minister the theological colleges were turning out. From what he had seen of them he judged that their pulpit manner was too stiff and unnatural, and as pastors they seemed to think they were too good for their flock. He did not want to become an unnatural, artificial minister like that. Finally, and most important, what was the will of God?

While he was thinking the matter over, he thought he distinctly heard a voice saying to him, *'Seekest thou great things for thyself? Seek them not!'* Spurgeon took it as a message from God himself, come at a crisis-point in his life. It made him realise that hitherto his desire to be a minister had been based on his own ambition and self-seeking. From now on he resolved to do only the work that God gave him to do. He would stay at Waterbeach.

As a part-timer at Waterbeach Spurgeon had little

time for pastoral visiting, although he made the most of his Sundays. Poor as the folk were, they were extremely hospitable, and he took his meals with each of the families in turn. Before long he had to give up his ushership in Cambridge. Now he had more time to devote to his pastorate, but he still had to make do on the forty-five pounds salary. His congregation helped him out as much as they could with gifts of food. He continued to live in Cambridge, partly because he hoped to open his own school there; meanwhile, he was sometimes so short of money that he paid his landlady with the bread and meat that his people brought in for him on market day.

Spurgeon's fame was spreading in Cambridgeshire, and he was becoming known as 'the Boy Preacher of the Fens'. He was invited to preach in other places, for special occasions such as church anniversaries. Sometimes the deacons who invited him were dismayed when they realised how very young he was. One or two were even rather rude to him. Spurgeon was not above delivering a reproof from the pulpit; often his wit and boldness disarmed his critics and made him some good friends.

He had some enemies, though, who were jealous of the success of this teenager, whom hundreds were flocking to hear. They doubted his honesty, too; he preached with such confidence, like a Christian with an advanced experience of the Faith, that they thought he must have 'cribbed' his sermons from some older person. In 1853 matters came to a head. Spurgeon was one of the three speakers invited to address the annual meeting of the Cambridge Sunday School Union. As the youngest he was called upon to speak first. He spoke in his usual direct and simple style, and was amazed to find that when the other two ministers took their turn they spoke of him slightingly and insultingly. Spurgeon asked leave of the chairman to reply to these attacks, and conducted his remarks with maturity and wisdom. One member of the audience was so impressed by his handling of the affair, as well as with his sermon at the beginning of the meeting, that a few days later he recommended that the deacons of New Park Street Chapel, London, should try to secure Spurgeon as their new pastor.

New Park Street Chapel had held an honourable place in Baptist history for about three hundred years. At least one of its pastors had suffered in the pillory for his faith. The building held twelve hundred people, but by the mid-nineteenth century the two hundred who gathered there seemed a woefully small number. Its situation in Southwark had deteriorated with passage of time. It was now surrounded by shabby houses, warehouses and factories, and the only direct road to it lay across Southwark Bridge, where a toll was charged. The deacons were desperately praying for a pastor who would restore the chapel's fortunes. Was the Boy Preacher the answer?

Spurgeon himself did not at first think so. He did not realise he was such a prodigy in the eyes of the world, and could not imagine how the London church had come to hear of him. He supposed that it was some mistake. The Waterbeach deacons guessed that it was no mistake; they had known that sooner or later some large church or other would take their beloved pastor. Spurgeon wrote in answer to the letter of invitation suggesting a date when he could go and preach in New Park Street Chapel. He also added − in case it had been a mistake after all −

'I have been wondering very much how you could have heard of me, and I think I ought to give some account of myself, lest I should come and be out of my right place. Although I have been more than two years minister of a church, which has in that time doubled, yet my last birthday was only my nineteenth, I have hardly ever known what the fear of man means, and have all but uniformly had large congregations, and frequently crowded ones, but if you think my years would unqualify me for your pulpit, then, by all means, I entreat you, do not let me come.'

As if any decaying church would have doubts of him, with such a record of preaching as that!

2 Mr Valiant-for-Truth
(1853 – 1858)

Spurgeon had an uncomfortable journey to London when he went to preach in New Park Street Chapel for the first time. It was the middle of December, and the cold weather only added to his shivers: he was already highly nervous about preaching in a big London church. He had been told to go to a boarding house in Queen Square, Bloomsbury; none of the Chapel members could or would offer him hospitality. At the boarding house lived a number of young men who fancied themselves as smart City types. They were greatly amused at the idea of the country bumpkin's aspiring to be a great London preacher, and spent the evening telling Spurgeon of all the great preachers London had seen, what great congregations they had had, and how learned they had been. The country pastor went to bed in a tiny, cheerless room, and was unable to sleep because of the roar of the London traffic.

On a clear, cold Sunday morning he made his way to Southwark. He felt very much alone in the 'dreary wilderness of brick' and was burdened by a sense of his own inadequacy. He prayed as he walked along, and soon began to feel that he was not alone, that God was at hand to help him. When he was actually in the pulpit and saw the congregation he felt better: '*By God's help I was not yet out of my depth, and was not likely to be with so small an audience.*'

The congregation approved of Spurgeon's preaching, although he *would* wave his handkerchief (a blue one, with spots). They called on their friends and acquaintances and urged them to come to the evening service. Many more turned up than had been there in the morning, and they were all delighted with the eloquence, zeal and knowledge of the young preacher. In fact, they hardly noticed the offending handkerchief. It was clear to the deacons that they must invite Spurgeon to preach again before long. After the service they arranged for him to come on three Sundays in the new year. Lest there be any misunderstanding Spurgeon told them frankly that he was not a College man. '*That is to us a special recommendation,*' they replied, '*for you would not have much savour or unction if you came from College.*' They had tried men from College, and had been bored stiff by their dry, intellectual pulpit style. Spurgeon's freshness, warmth and earnestness was just what they wanted.

Before the end of January 1854 – before Spurgeon had even completed the three Sundays' preaching – a church meeting was called at New Park Street Chapel, at which it was resolved to invite him to be their pastor for a trial period of six months. Spurgeon was happy to accept, but not for so long a period. In view of his youthfulness he felt it wiser to agree to preach at Southwark for three months only. If things went well between himself and the congregation a further three months could be agreed as an extension of the trial period. But he would not commit himself to six months from the outset.

In fact there was no need for a six months' probation. He began his temporary pastorate in the February, and by April it was clear to both church and pastor that they suited each other. Spurgeon was particularly pleased with the Monday evening prayer meetings, which were always well attended. They demonstrated to him that the people of Southwark would support him with their prayers – something he cared about more than money. For their part the regular chapel-goers had the satisfaction of seeing the building filled and souls converted. On the twenty-eighth of April 1854 Spurgeon accepted a formal invitation to the permanent pastorship. He held the position for thirty-eight years, until his death.

Spurgeon saw his new environment of Southwark very much as a mission field, but over and above that he was called to be a pastor, to care for the souls of the Christians who worshipped in his church. He was faced with one pastoral problem quite soon after his appointment; a man came to see him claiming that he had left the church because of the way he had been treated by various prominent members. Spurgeon listened patiently to his tale of wrongs, and noticed that this man spoke badly of people he himself had found to be honest and caring. So he told him that now the church had a new pastor the best thing would be for everyone to forget the past and begin again. It was a policy he stuck to: he would have nothing to do with old quarrels, and avoided involvement with any cliques or rivalries that had grown up before his time. So successful was this policy that the church remained united for the whole of his pastorate.

Asiatic cholera broke out in London in 1854, and the young pastor spent weary months visiting the sick and comforting the dying. He gave up all engagements to preach away from London, and concentrated his efforts on Southwark and the surrounding area. Many of his congregation suffered, and day after day he saw his friends dying. He threw himself into the work at first, but before long he became thoroughly depressed. It was hard to be at the bedside of a dying member of his church, but harder still to be called to someone who had mocked and jeered at his preaching, and who was now too near to death to receive the Good News Spurgeon could have given him.

Once the outbreak was over, however, the pastor's natural cheerfulness returned, and the congregation of New Park Street Chapel began to increase once more. At first its members simply invited their friends to come along and hear their remarkable preacher. But a crowd attracts a crowd. On one occasion an alcoholic was attracted into the building by the sight of the crowds entering; on another it was a prostitute on her way to throw herself from Blackfriars Bridge. Each time Spurgeon, in the course of the sermon, spoke words that seemed to describe just their situation. They were convinced that God was speaking directly to them, and were converted.

At his first invitation to New Park Street the deacons had mentioned to Spurgeon the number of young people who came to the chapel, and for whom they hoped he would have a particular care. As a 'young person' himself he could be expected to have a wide sympathy for them. One of these young people was the twenty-two year old Susannah Thompson. She was related to Mr Olney, one of the deacons, and had attended the chapel with his family since she was a little girl. As a child she had been fascinated by the pulpit, which was rather like a great swallow's nest attached to the wall. It was entered through a door at the back, and Susannah could never actually see the minister coming into the pulpit. He just appeared as if by magic. When Charles Spurgeon became pastor of the church the interest she felt in the pulpit soon extended to its occupant.

'Susie', as she was generally known, had become a Christian about a year earlier, but had told nobody about it. The first excitement of her new relationship with God soon left her, and she lost interest in prayer and Bible reading. Under the preaching of Spurgeon, however, she began to wake up, and soon she became alarmed at her own spiritual apathy. She consulted William Olney, one of the deacon's sons, and received help and encouragement from him. He must have mentioned Susie to the Pastor, for she was surprised to receive from Spurgeon the gift of an illustrated copy of *The Pilgrim's Progress*. She was very impressed by this evidence of his concern for her, and soon found herself able to confide to him the difficulties she had been having. Through his preaching and counselling she was brought to rededicate herself as a Christian.

A friendship developed between the two, but Susie was slow to realise that Charles had a more than friendly interest in her. The opening of the Crystal Palace at Sydenham on the tenth of June 1854, was the occasion he chose to turn her thoughts towards marriage. They sat with a large party of friends, waiting for the procession to pass by and meanwhile talking and laughing amongst themselves. Charles had a copy of Martin Tupper's *Proverbial Philosophy*. Opening it at the chapter on marriage, he showed Susie the lines,

> *'If thou art to have a wife of thy youth, she is now living on the earth;*
> *Therefore think of her, and pray for her weal.'*

'Do you pray for him who is to be your husband?' he whispered in Susie's ear. When the time came for the visitors to look round at the Palace and its gardens, the couple escaped from the rest of their party and walked together, their friendship ripening into love. In the

August Charles proposed to Susie, and she accepted.

Susie was now assiduous in attending the services at New Park Street Chapel, and on the first of February 1855 she was baptised there by her fiancé. The lovers met as often as they could. They frequently went to the Crystal Palace, and always waited for each other at the Crystal Fountain. Charles usually visited the Thompsons' home on a Monday. He had already begun the publishing of his sermons, and would bring along his Sunday's sermon to revise it for the press. Susie learned to sit quietly by, giving him the pleasure of her company but not her voice, until he had finished. It was the only way Charles could fit in his courting with his pastoral work. Susie at first found it hard to have to give way so much to Charles' work as a minister, but she was to admit later that it was a valuable discipline for her. She spent most of her married life as an invalid, and had to remain behind the scenes while Charles was in the public eye, and travelling extensively.

Early in his career Spurgeon was preaching to crowds who filled New Park Street Chapel to overflowing. This brought some problems. The Chapel windows were not made to open, and in the evenings, when the gas lights were on, the atmosphere was stifling. Spurgeon remarked several times to his deacons that the top window panes ought to be removed, but nothing was done until

'It providentially happened, one Monday, that somebody removed most of those panes . . . There

*was considerable consternation, and much
conjecture, as to who had committed the crime, and
I proposed that a reward of five pounds should be
offered for the discovery of the offender . . . I have
not felt it to be my duty to inform against the
individual. I trust none will suspect me, but if they
do, I shall have to confess that I have walked with
the stick which let the oxygen into that stifling
structure.'*

At the end of August 1854 the church meeting decided
to extend the Chapel. There were legal delays, but the
extension was begun early in 1855, with a new school-
room being built alongside the chapel; windows between could be lowered to allow those in the school-
room to hear what was going on in the Chapel.

While the alterations were in progress the church
moved to Exeter Hall in the Strand. It could hold
about four and a half thousand people, and had hitherto been used mainly by the Sacred Harmonic Society.
The Hall was booked for eight successive Sundays,
then, as the alterations were not complete, for eight
more. The change of venue brought Spurgeon's
preaching into the public eye as never before. Every
Sunday, morning and evening, Exeter Hall was filled
and crowds blocked the Strand. The strain on Spurgeon was terrific. In his earnest pleadings with sinners
to come to Christ, or in his elevated praise of God, his
voice would almost fail. He sometimes had recourse to
a glass of Chili-vinegar – a painful way to restore his
voice! Later he developed a silver tone which was

peculiarly sweet and piercing, and he was able to speak without difficulty to thousands, indoors or out.

Up to this time references to Spurgeon in the press had been limited to comments in religious newspapers (it should be borne in mind, though, that many of these were widely read). Now the preacher came to the notice of the popular press. *The Ipswich Express* published an article about the meetings in Exeter Hall under the headline 'A Clerical Poltroon', in which it said,

> *'All his discourses are redolent of bad taste, are vulgar and theatrical, and yet he is so run after that, unless you go half-an-hour before the time, you will not be able to get in at all . . . I hear, the other Sunday, the gifted divine had the impudence, before preaching, to say, as there were many young ladies present, that he was engaged – that his heart was another's, he wished them clearly to understand that – that he might have no presents sent him, no attentions paid him, no worsted slippers worked for him by the young ladies present.'*

In the face of complaints of libel from some of Spurgeon's friends, the paper had to back down and admit that the article had been written from hearsay, and without sight or hearing of any of Spurgeon's sermons. It eventually gave a review of two sermons and dismissed the preacher in these terms:

> *'There is enough foolishness in London to keep up,
> in flourishing style, Tom Thumb, Charles Keen, the
> Living Skeleton, C. H. Spurgeon, and many other
> delusions all at once, and yet to allow a vast mass of
> sober minded citizens to go "the even tenor of their
> way", quite unaffected by such transient turmoils.'*

But it was too late to suppress the story of 'the slippers'. The lie was taken up by other newspapers and repeated so often that it came to be believed; some people even said they had actually heard Spurgeon utter the words attributed to him. All sorts of other tales were attaching themselves to him too. Common pulpit anecdotes took on a new life when attributed to C. H. Spurgeon. He was supposed to have slid down the banister of his pulpit in order to show how easy it is to 'backslide' from the Faith — and that at a time when his pulpit had no banisters! Of press reports Spurgeon wrote that,

> *'When my personal habits are truthfully reported,
> though they are really not the concern of anybody
> but myself, I feel utterly indifferent about it . . . I
> am quite willing to take my fair share of the current
> criticism allotted to public men, but I cannot help
> saying that I very seldom read in print any story
> connected with myself has a shade of truth in it . . .
> tales of remotest and fustiest antiquity are imputed
> to me as they have been to men who went before me,
> and will be to men who follow after.'*

43

He found it relatively easy to ignore the jibes of the popular press: the overall result was that interest was roused in him and his work, more people came to hear him – and went away converted. It was much harder, however, to stomach the sneers and backbiting of the religious world. A member of his own denomination, the successful Baptist preacher James Wells, set the tone by an insulting and patronising article which questioned the 'Divine reality' of Spurgeon's own conversion, and complained that his preaching was deceiving all those who thought they were converted by it. Spurgeon himself did his best to ignore such attacks. His interests did not lie with the religious world as such. He wanted to contact those who were not religious – the slum-dwellers, the drunkards and the prostitutes of Southwark. What was said as a criticism was received by him as an accolade, that

> *'The greater part of the multitude that weekly crowd to his theatrical exhibitions consists of people who are not in the habit of frequenting a place of worship.'*

After all his hard work at Exeter Hall Spurgeon felt in need of a holiday, and decided to go to Scotland in July. He had several preaching engagements in Scotland for that month, and thought that he could take a working holiday. It turned out to be the very worst of ideas. He could not relax completely in the brief periods between his engagements, and consequently his preaching suffered. Nevertheless he found himself addressing thousands, while many others were turned away. No doubt those who invited him counted these meetings a great success. Spurgeon himself was not so sure. He missed Susie dreadfully, and had to admit that now he knew how *she* felt when his work took him from her. He judged that he was in poor spiritual shape, and asked Susie to pray for him:

> '*I fear I am not so full of love to God as I used to be. I lament my sad decline in spiritual things . . . Oh! what is it to be popular, to be successful, to have abundance, even to have love so sweet as yours – if I should be left of God to fall, and to depart from His ways?*'

Glowing accounts of his work were appearing in the Scottish papers, but he could not feel flattered by them – he felt too keenly that he was not right spiritually, and that any success must be attributed directly to God. Looking back on it later, he saw that this depression was God's way of preserving him from self-conceit.

Such a clamour of popularity (and notoriety) was very trying to him in these early years. He was very conscious of the temptation to vainglory that accompanied his position as a star attraction, and prayed often and earnestly to be kept from pride. As we have just seen, his prayer was sometimes answered in a way that was very uncomfortable for him. In a sense it was easy for Spurgeon to be humble, because the temptation was such an obvious one, but on some occasions the quickness of his wit in answering a criticism or in meeting an awkward situation gave him a satisfaction that bordered even on smugness. He considered his mental agility as a weapon to be used in the service of his Lord, and use it he would – whether to comfort a despairing soul, or to snub someone who thought too well of himself. People with him fell into two categories: either they were in need of God's love and grace, or they were brothers and sisters in Christ. His two great aims in life were to preach the Gospel to the former, and to instruct and edify the latter. With these overriding claims upon his energies, it is not surprising that he seems not always to have met people on equal ground, with love and respect for the individual as he was. His role as pastor dominated his relationship with others.

Charles and Susie were married on the eighth of January 1856, at New Park Street Chapel. The place was packed to overflowing with a crowd of eager admirers – rather like the crowd that assembles outside the registry office for the marriage of a modern pop star! The honeymoon was spent in Paris, a city that Susie knew quite well. She had spent a few months in the home of a French pastor, as a part of her education. She and Charles spent ten days in a whirl of cultural activity, visiting the Louvre, Versailles, la Madeleine and Notre Dame. Of the many Roman Catholic churches they visited Susie wrote,

> 'We always found something to admire, though, alas! there was also much to deplore.'

They came home to number 217 New Kent Road, a neat terraced house where they had a front parlour, but decided to use the drawing-room as a study for Charles. They could not afford luxuries; in fact they kept to a 'rigid economy'. The reason for this was that Spurgeon was paying for the education of a young man, T. W. Medhurst, who wanted to be a minister. He was quite uneducated, and some of 'The very precise friends who were at that time members of New Park Street' wanted him stopped as a disgrace to the cause. Medhurst himself admitted that his English was bad, and that he made mistakes, but insisted that he must preach. The only solution was to give him the education he needed. Spurgeon sent him to a Baptist Collegiate School for his basics, and himself spent several hours a week teaching him theology. In this small way Pastor's College (now Spurgeon's College) began its existence. More young men, wanting to preach the gospel, asked for help, and soon the work had to be put on a regular basis. Spurgeon asked his friend George Rogers, an Independent minister, to be the Principal. The eight students the College began with lodged at Mr Rogers'; additions to the College boarded with members of the church.

Spurgeon was always more than generous with his money, and to make sure they had enough for household expenses Susie never ran up a bill, but paid for everything as she bought it. Even so, on one occasion they found they had a large bill to pay – for rates or taxes – and nothing to pay it with. They wondered how they might raise the money; Spurgeon suggested that he do without the horse and carriage that he hired, but Susie was against that idea. Charles had to go so often to the Chapel to conduct services that, although they did not live much more than a mile from New Park Street, Susie was sure the walking would be too much for him. They discussed the matter anxiously, and prayed about it. Within twenty-four hours they received a letter containing a gift of twenty-four pounds which the anonymous donor stipulated was to be for Spurgeon's own use, not for the Chapel. This was the first of many such answers to prayer; it gave Spurgeon such confidence in God's providence that he was never again anxious about finding money for the projects he had in mind.

Although their home was very small (by Victorian standards) they never felt it to be so — except when Susie was anxiously waiting for Charles to return from a distant preaching engagement. Then she would feel cramped in the tiny parlour, and would pace up and down in the narrow hall, until she heard the cab draw up outside. After his Sunday's preaching Spurgeon would often find himself both tired and excited. The best thing to soothe and relax him, he found, was for him to listen while Susie read to him. Sometimes she read from George Herbert's poems, at other times from Baxter's *Reformed Pastor*.

Spurgeon always prepared his Sunday sermons on the Saturday. Since the Cambridge days he had been used to preparing himself only a few hours before he was to preach. He liked the immediacy of such a procedure: he could preach on whatever topic seemed most appropriate for the circumstances of his hearers. Although he was generally confident as to what topic he should preach about, he was not always sure about the text he should take as his starting-point. The Bible seemed to be so full of good texts that it was difficult to choose the best!

Although he cherished the feeling of spontaneity in his sermons, only once did he actually preach without any preparation whatsoever. He had in fact a sermon-outline before him in his pulpit at New Park Street, but as he opened his Bible to read out the text, his eye fell upon a verse on the opposite page which *'Sprang upon me, like a lion from a thicket, with vastly more power than I had felt when considering the text I had chosen.'* The congregation was singing the last verse of a hymn, and Spurgeon had only a minute or two in which to make up his mind: should he stick to his original plan, or should he take this new text and preach on that, as being given to him by God for this occasion? He chose the latter course, and began to preach extempore, without notes. But he could only think of two main points to draw from this particular passage: how the sermon was going to end he had no idea. He got to the end of his second point, and was just wondering whether he should end the service early, when the gas lights went out, and the chapel was plunged in darkness. There was danger of panic, for the aisles were crowded as usual. Spurgeon was able to quiet the congregation by telling them that the gas would soon be relit, and that meanwhile, as he was preaching without notes, he could go on in the dark, if they would just keep still and listen. Now he spoke on spiritual darkness and spiritual light, finding no lack of things to say. A few months later two people asked to become members of the Chapel; both had been converted that evening, one by the discourse before the lamps went out, the other by that given afterwards.

A different test of his spontaneity and ingenuity occurred when Spurgeon was invited one Sunday to preach at Haverhill, Suffolk, not far from Stambourne. Owing to a breakdown on the railway he was late, and arrived at the little chapel to find that the sermon had already been started – by no less a person than his own grandfather! As Charles made his way up the aisle the old man broke off his discourse (he was preaching on the text, *'For by grace are ye saved through faith; and that not of yourselves: it is the gift of God'*) and exclaimed *'Here comes my grandson! He may preach the gospel better than I can, but he cannot preach a better gospel; can you, Charles?'* Charles replied, *'You can preach better than I can. Pray go on.'* But the old man insisted that Charles should preach and so he did, taking up just where his grandfather had left off. But when he began to develop the theme of the weakness of human nature, in illustration of *'And that not of yourselves'*, the old man pulled his coat-tails and said, *'I know most about that.'* So he dealt with the depravity of human nature and the awfulness of the human condition, then allowed Charles to continue on 'The gift of God'. Once he said, 'Tell them that again, Charles' – so of course Charles did tell them it again; and he could never afterwards read that text without seeming to hear his grandfather's voice exhorting him to *'Tell them that again'*.

The extension to New Park Street Chapel proved to be a waste of time and money. It was impossible to contain all the church members, let alone those who came casually, just to hear the famous preacher. So at a church meeting in May 1856 it was decided that Exeter Hall should be hired again, this time for Sunday evenings only. However, the church found it very inconvenient to be meeting in Southwark in the mornings and the Strand in the evenings. In August a committee was formed and a Fund begun for the provision of a much larger church building. At about the same time the owners of Exeter Hall let it be known that they were not prepared to let the building exclusively to the Baptists. New Park Street congregation therefore had to find somewhere else for the evenings until their new chapel could be built – which would not be for several years.

Somebody suggested the Music Hall in the Royal Surrey Gardens might be an appropriate place. Spurgeon went with William Olney to look at it. The Hall held up to ten thousand people. Spurgeon and Olney felt that, though it seemed a 'venturesome experiment' to take on such a large building, they should nevertheless have faith that God would bless their endeavours. A few members of the church were shocked at the very idea of preaching in what they called 'the devil's house'. The hall had been built in the Surrey Gardens (which also contained a menagerie) for the performance of 'popular concerts'. These were, of course, what would nowadays be called 'music hall' affairs, with plenty of impropriety and vulgarity. Spurgeon was not put off by the objections of the few, but encouraged them to dissociate themselves from the proceedings. They did not have to violate their consciences by going; he did not intend to violate his by abandoning the project. The Music Hall was engaged for a trial period of one month, beginning on the nineteenth of October, and a licence was obtained for the use of the place for Dissenting worship.

On the morning of the nineteenth Spurgeon preached in New Park Street Chapel, on a verse from the prophet Malachi – *'Prove me now'*. The congregation was excited, and expecting great things for the evening. Spurgeon himself felt burdened with a sense of responsibility, and *'Filled with a mysterious premonition of some great trial shortly to befall me.'* He urged the church to have faith in the power of God to save souls, even those of the idle, the blasphemous and the scoffing, many of whom would surely be at the Music Hall that evening.

> *'See what God can do, just when a cloud is falling on the head of him whom God had raised up to preach to you, go and prove him now, and see if He will not pour you out such a blessing as ye had not even dreamed of . . . '*

Spurgeon did not then know how prophetic his words were, or just what sort of cloud it was that was about to fall upon him.

That evening Spurgeon made his way to the Music Hall, and was surprised to find the streets thronged with people for some distance. The drive itself, from the gate of the Gardens to the Hall, was one solid block of people unable to get into the building. It was estimated that more than seven thousand people were inside, and an equal number around the outside of the building, wanting to get in. There was no point in waiting until the advertised time; Spurgeon began the service ten minutes early.

Proceedings were scarcely under way when a commotion broke out near the doorway. Cries of *'Fire!'* were heard, *'The galleries are giving way!' 'The place is falling!'* A panic ensued, with a stampede for the exit. According to an eyewitness account,

> *'the people in the galleries rushed down, precipitating themselves almost headlong over, or breaking down the balustrade of the stairs, killing some and fearfully wounding others. Those who fell through force, or fainting, were trampled underfoot, and several lives were lost in the mêlée.'*

Spurgeon tried to calm the audience, assuring them as loudly and as calmly as possible that there was no fire, and the building was quite safe. Those nearest the pulpit, unaware of the seriousness of the disturbance, called for him to preach. Things became quieter and Spurgeon, quite ignorant that some people had actually died, began to speak about the suddenness and nearness of death. But the clamour broke out again, and he was forced to stop. He announced a hymn, and begged the congregation to make an orderly exit while it was being sung. He had done his best to appear unperturbed, but he was deeply distressed by the knowledge of the panic and a growing fear that people had been killed. He had only the strength to pronounce the Benediction before he collapsed, and was carried from the Hall. A deacon dashed to New Kent Road to tell Susie of the disaster, and to warn her that her husband was being brought home. She had given birth to twin sons just a month earlier, and was still in need of rest and quiet, but she rose to the occasion and did all in her power to comfort her husband. He would not be comforted, however, and in the morning she began to fear for his sanity. The deacons decided that the family should move to the house of one of their number, Mr Winsor, who lived in the suburb of Croydon. Charles was ten days there in a state of nervous depression before he finally recovered.

Seven people were killed in the disaster, and at least 28 badly injured. The Chapel opened a fund for the relief of the sufferers and their dependents. An inquest was held, and a verdict of accidental death was brought. In fact, many of the New Park Street congregation believed that the panic had been started deliberately. One eyewitness even stated that *'The thing bore the impress of a plan to which some hundreds of persons at least appeared to be parties.'* While it is quite likely that some individuals shouted *'Fire!'* in a malicious spirit, it is wholly improbable that several hundred were involved in a conspiracy. The reckless crowding of the building, together with the total lack of emergency exits, are almost enough in themselves to account for the panic. But the Victorians had very little experience of dealing with enormous crowds of people in public buildings, and nobody supposed that either New Park Street Chapel, as the organisers of the meeting, or the owners of the Music Hall, could be really to blame.

Spurgeon had not sought publicity but he got it now. He became a national figure, and before long Spurgeon and his monster evangelistic services became something of a tourist attraction. Journalists actually went to hear the preacher for themselves, and some papers changed their tune and began to write in praise of him.

Services at the Surrey Gardens were resumed from the twenty-third of November, in the mornings only. There was less danger of fire, or of any other outbreak, in the daylight hours. Many distinguished people came to hear the famous preacher, including the Princess Royal, Lord Palmerston and Florence Nightingale. With a congregation that included the poorest and the wealthiest in London, Spurgeon at first found it difficult to strike a balance in his preaching, so that he could appeal to all hearers. As time went on, however, his audience contained an increasing number of those who had been converted, and he felt that he should give some further teaching on the Christian's growing understanding of his faith, and his developing relationship with God. He adjusted his sermons accordingly. One result of this was that most of Spurgeon's converts did not drift away, but joined the church and became active members of the fellowship.

Although a convinced Calvinist himself, Spurgeon fell foul of the more rigid souls – the hyper-Calvinists – who took offence at his general invitation to all who would, to come and be saved. They particularly disliked one sermon he preached, on Jesus' words in the parable, *'Compel them to come in'*, complaining that it was *'Arminian and unsound'*. But many people were converted through that sermon, so Spurgeon took very little notice of his critics. He actually pursued a middle ground between the Calvinistic belief that God determines everything, including man's thoughts and actions, and the Arminian belief that man is a free agent, with responsibility for his own actions:

> *'If I were to declare that man was so free to act that there was no control of God over his actions, I should be driven very near to atheism; and if, on the other hand, I should declare that God so over-rules all things that man is not free enough to be responsible, I should be driven at once into Antinomianism or fatalism. That God predestines, and yet that man is responsible, are two facts that few can see clearly. They are believed to be inconsistent and contradictory, but they are not. The fault is in our weak judgment.'*

Spurgeon's middle view did not placate his critics;

while the hyper-Calvinists accused him of Arminianism, the Arminianists accused him of hyper-Calvinism!

The Arminian/hyper-Calvinist dispute was only a minor irritation to Spurgeon. He was more troubled because a large section of the British Church was neglecting to teach the truths of the Gospel, and was wandering off into what seemed to him a vague area of noble thoughts and good intentions. The cross of Christ seemed to have no place in the religion of many: it was simply a matter of good deeds and a vague aspiration after God. He was not surprised therefore, only saddened, when a controversy arose in the religious press over a book of hymns entitled *The Rivulet, or Hymns for the Heart and Voice.* It was published in 1856 by T. T. Lynch. Various papers reviewed the volume favourably, but the (evangelical) *Morning Advertiser* condemned it for its lack of vital Christianity. Thereupon fifteen of the leading London ministers signed a protest in which they commended *'the literary and devotional merits of the hymns, as well as the orthodoxy of their author.'* The debate was becoming acrimonious when Spurgeon was asked to review *The Rivulet* for *The Christian Cabinet.* He gave his opinion that the book was not really worth all the excitement: as poetry it was not a masterpiece, but was unexceptionable; as a hymnbook it was quite unsuitable for public worship; theologically there was not enough in it to pronounce judgment. What troubled him more was that the ministers had risen in its defence. They should be spending their time opposing what was clearly false doctrine. *'As long as the fight is thought to be concerning a book,'* he concluded, *'the issue is doubtful, but let it be for God and for his truth, and the battle is the Lord's . . . the apostle of the Son of God bids you stand fast in the liberty wherewith* Christ *has made you free. THE OLD FAITH MUST BE TRIUMPHANT.'*

In 1857 the Spurgeon family moved to Nightingale Lane, Clapham, which ran alongside a large private park. Facing the park were a few scattered houses, one of which, 'Helensburgh', was bought by the Spurgeons. They could just afford to buy it with the income from the sale of Spurgeon's sermons as well as an increase in salary the Chapel had just awarded him. It was an old house with a large garden, but had been unoccupied for a long time. Setting to rights the dusty rooms and neglected garden was a lengthy task which afforded many hours of enjoyment and relaxation to the little family. As the twins Charles and Thomas grew bigger, they wanted to help in the various jobs to be done about the house. Their father gave them a basket of tools and a box of nails – and thoughtfully provided a roll of clean rag for them to use as bandages! He arranged for one of the College students to act as their tutor, and the boys liked to consider themselves as part of the College.

Susie was now free to devote her attention to her husband's well-being. She called him her Tirshatha, a title used of the governor of Judaea under the Persian empire. It meant 'Your Excellency'. In these early years Susie enjoyed good health, and was able to accompany her husband on preaching trips or on holiday. It was her delight to care for his welfare and to nurse him when he was ill. He had quite a serious illness in 1858, and was visited at Clapham by John Ruskin. Ruskin was still on good terms with the Evangelicals, for he had not then been troubled with the difficulties and doubts of his later years. He often went to the Surrey Music Hall, and was a keen admirer of Spurgeon. He brought with him two engravings and some bottles of wine as a cordial for the patient. Spurgeon was touched by the love and consideration shown in the visit and the gifts. He remembered it with appreciation in the later years when Ruskin repudiated much of what Spurgeon believed in.

3   The Governor
(1858 – 1892)

The Committee formed in 1856 worked for two years gathering funds for the new church building, which was to be called the Metropolitan Tabernacle. Members of the church gave week by week, sometimes quite small sums of money – but all gave as much as they were able. A large proportion of the money was raised by Spurgeon himself. He began midweek lectures, for which a fee was charged, and gave the proceeds to the building fund. Although he made sure that most of his Sundays were spent at the Music Hall and New Park Street, he preached at many other churches during the week. Often the entire collection was donated to the Building Fund. In these cases Spurgeon made a point of going back after a year and preaching once more. This time the collection would be donated to a local cause. By the middle of 1858 the church had enough money to buy a freehold site for the new Tabernacle. A tedious search for a suitable plot followed, but by December the committee had found a site at Newington which they could purchase for five thousand pounds.

Plans for the new building were drawn up in the Grecian style: Spurgeon preferred this to the Gothic as being more appropriate to Christianity, the Greek language being that of the New Testament. The foundation stone was laid by Sir Samuel Morton Peto (later Lord Somerleyton) on the sixteenth of August 1859, in the presence of about three thousand people.

In December the last service was held in the Music Hall. The proprietors wanted to open the Gardens for Sunday entertainment, and the Christians had to leave. They returned to Exeter Hall for a further, cramped fifteen months. How they looked forward to the time when the Tabernacle would be completed!

The very first meeting to be held in the new building was in the summer of 1860. At this meeting Spurgeon gave an account of the Continental tour he and Susie had just made — their first real holiday since their honeymoon. A high point of the trip had been when Spurgeon preached in Geneva Cathedral, in Calvin's pulpit. That was the only occasion he ever donned clerical dress; he usually wore a black coat and a white bow-tie. The Tabernacle was still hardly more than a shell, however, and the meeting had been called, not just to hear about the holiday, but to discuss how to fund the rest of the work. Inspired by their pastor's enthusiasm and liberality, the church members made a further effort and, sure enough, when the Tabernacle was completed in 1861, at a total cost of twenty thousand pounds, there were no debts outstanding. It was opened on the eighteenth of March with an early morning prayer meeting at which more than a thousand people were present. True to the church's expectation its membership expanded rapidly; seventy-two people asked to join at the first (monthly) church meeting, with similar increases in the succeeding months.

The eight theological students were now able to use the Tabernacle schoolrooms for their studies. Spurgeon had several more men wanting to join 'Pastor's College', and found himself quite unable to support them all. Hitherto he had contributed six to eight hundred pounds annually out of his own pocket. The large sales of his sermons in the United States had gone a long way to raising this amount, but in 1860 demand suddenly dropped. Spurgeon was not surprised: he had included denunciations of slavery in several sermons and letters to the American press, knowing that this would offend many of his readers in the Southern States. But he could do without the American revenue, for it was time his own congregation was offered a share of the work. At a church meeting in July the church formally undertook responsibility for the College. Soon there were sixteen full-time students, with eleven part-timers coming to evening classes.

Numbers were to increase even more as time went on.

Spurgeon always devoted his Fridays to the College: he would prepare a talk in the morning, after he had dealt with his correspondence, and deliver it to the students in the afternoon. With a sympathetic and intelligent audience he could really let himself go, and for two hours he would talk with great wit and wisdom on aspects of a minister's work. The best of these talks were later collected and published in three volumes under the title of *Lectures to my Students.* In them he seems more relaxed and at ease, more the man among his equals and less the pastor with his flock than in any of his sermons.

The sermons, as have been noted, were aimed at converting the unbeliever and instructing the young convert. Spurgeon was not given to narrow denominationalism; he was aware of the beliefs and attitudes of those in other churches, and was glad to be a member of the Evangelical Alliance. This was an association which aimed at drawing together evangelical opinion from both Established Church and Dissent. It laid emphasis on the beliefs evangelicals had in common, although it could be said that it deliberately ignored points where there was known to be disagreement. The Alliance was particularly anxious to keep harmony between evangelicals in order to present a united front to the Anglo-Catholics.

Since the 1840's the Tractarian Movement had appealed to the Book of Common Prayer to show that as Anglicans they were right in viewing the Church as the only vehicle of God's revelation to man, and that salvation was only to be had through the 'means of grace' administered by the church – that is, through the sacraments of communion and baptism. The Evangelical Alliance was totally opposed to such beliefs, seeing them as 'creeping Popery'. However, it was hampered in expressing its opposition because the Anglican half of its members drew their doctrines from the same Prayer Book as the Tractarians. Before long the whole issue was bogged down in a debate over what the sixteenth-century Reformers had meant when they formulated the Thirty-nine Articles.

Up to 1864 Spurgeon had taken little notice of the Tractarian Movement; but then it suddenly dawned upon him that it was making great advances among Anglican clergymen. From Anglo-Catholicism it was an easy step to Roman Catholicism, particularly with the Tractarian understanding of the Prayer Book. So in June and July 1864 Spurgeon departed from his usual pulpit style and in three sermons launched a public attack on the Prayer Book. The first was on *Baptismal Regeneration*, in which he accused evangelical Anglicans of compromising with Anglo-Catholicism when they accepted the Prayer Book service of Baptism. The charge annoyed them, and many took to pen and paper in order to say so. A great number of pamphlets was issued, and the affair became a full-scale controversy when Spurgeon preached two more sermons, one entitled, *'Let us go Forth'*, in which he called for evangelicals to leave the Church of England, and the last with the title *'Thus saith the Lord: or the Book of Common Prayer weighed in the Balances of the Sanctuary'.* In this he discussed the authority of the Prayer Book and that of the Bible, and gave seven instances of the Prayer Book's being without the authority of the Bible. He accused evangelical Anglicans of a duplicity not even practised by the Tractarians.

Many Anglicans opposed Spurgeon not so much because they defended baptismal regeneration, but in exasperation at the tone of his remarks. They felt that he had betrayed the cause of evangelical unity. They were convinced that the Reformers only meant to imply that baptism becomes a means of grace when it is rightly received, in the atmosphere of a Christian home and family. In fact, Article twenty-five went so far as to deny that the saving influences of the Holy Spirit accompanied every administration of the sacrament. Many Anglican evangelicals felt that by weakening faith in the Church of England Spurgeon had actually helped the Anglo-Catholic cause. On the other hand Spurgeon was convinced that Anglo-Catholicism could only be effectively opposed on the basis of the Bible: the Prayer Book and the Establishment had to be jettisoned.

The Secretary of the Evangelical Alliance wrote to Spurgeon saying that he should either withdraw his harsh remarks or withdraw himself from the Alliance. He chose the latter course, but without animosity. Of Anglicans he could write,

> *'I can never forget the many gracious and faithful men who remain in this Church, nor can I cease to*

*pray for them. Towards these brethren, as earnest
adherents and promulgators of evangelical truth, I
sincerely cherish the warmest love.'*

His strong words from the pulpit were intended not as
insults but as an earnest warning to those he felt were
basing their conduct more on the wisdom of men than
of God. Nevertheless his participation in controversy
was not entirely judicious. He over-reacted to what he
saw as error, and over-simplified the issues involved.
He was much more successful devoting his time and
energy to the needs of his rapidly increasing church at
the Tabernacle.

As the church grew, so did the range of its labours.
It had a large fund for the relief of poverty, which
needed careful administration. Almshouses were built
for elderly women, and Ragged Schools for the care
and education of destitute children. Then there were
Sunday Schools, Day Schools, Societies for giving out
tracts and for making clothes for the poor, and the
Evangelists' Association. Spurgeon encouraged the
establishment of 'mission stations' in the slums of
South London; many College students began their
careers as ministers by working in such 'stations' until
they had gathered a congregation large enough to war-
rant the building of a chapel.

The Tabernacle had nine deacons, who were elec-
ted for life. These men were in effect the managers of
the church, dealing with all the business of running
such a large concern. In most Baptist chapels the
deacons were expected to be spiritual leaders too, but

in 1859 it became apparent that at the Tabernacle there were too few deacons to exercise total responsibility in both practical and spiritual matters. It was decided to revive the office of 'elder', and twenty-five men were appointed. They were to make pastoral visits, keeping an eye open for any member of the flock who seemed to be having difficulties, and promoting the spiritual welfare of all.

Spurgeon's was the mind behind these changes. He had a genius for organisation, and for choosing the right people to whom he could delegate responsibility. He was the leader of a team of workers who shared the burden of the Tabernacle. They all cheerfully acknowledged his leadership and often referred to him as 'the Governor'. The deacons too had their nicknames. There was the 'Son of Ali', 'Uncle Tom' and 'Prince Charlie', among others. Spurgeon inspired a genuine devotion in them, so much so that on one occasion when he spoke sharply to one of them in rebuke for some fault, he got the reply, *'Well, that may be so, but I tell you what, sir, I would die for you any day.'* With an answer like that Spurgeon had to apologise for his sharpness. He was inclined to be hasty in his reactions to people, and this sometimes led him to speak with undue acerbity. As he grew older he became aware of this fault, and tried to correct it. To his people it was all part of the great naturalness of their pastor. Whatever he said or did, he did it with such enthusiasm, such care for their wellbeing, that they readily forgave his faults. To them he seemed a guileless and wholehearted person.

It was characteristic of him that he should be a glutton for work, getting through more in a week than two or three of his helpers put together. He needed to be free of the administration and, to a lesser extent, the pastoral work of the Tabernacle so that he could throw himself into the work that only he could do – studying, preaching, preparing oral and printed sermons, and dealing with an ever-growing correspondence. For this last he employed a secretary, but he tried to write at least a few words to every individual who wrote to him, in the belief that this would give pleasure. He took his responsibilities as a public figure seriously. He found it almost impossible to refuse requests to preach in other towns and churches, and took on an incredible workload, often preaching ten times in one week. He literally drove himself to death; his early demise is largely attributable to overwork.

Sunday was, of course, Spurgeon's busiest day, with two services to conduct and hundreds of people to speak to. Many came after the services for advice and counselling; many more simply wanted to speak to him and to shake his hand. He was always ready to shake hands, for he wanted to get as near to his people as possible. Too many ministers cultivated a superior attitude and kept themselves aloof from their flock. This, to Spurgeon's mind, was largely the reason for their empty churches.

His Sunday morning sermon was published every following Thursday, and he always carefully revised his manuscript, improving his style and omitting any infelicities of expression. He would check the printer's proofs with equal care. He often wrote articles for the religious press, particularly for the *Baptist Messenger,* to which he had contributed since 1854. In 1865 he decided to start his own monthly magazine, *The Sword and the Trowel.* The title was taken from the account in the book of Nehemiah of the rebuilding of Jerusalem by the Jews: because of the threat of enemy attack the builders carried their weapons as they worked. Spurgeon wanted his magazine to be a vital weapon in attacking evil as well as a tool for the conversion of many. It was the organ of the Tabernacle, giving reports of the progress made in its many departments, informing readers of new projects to be supported by prayer and by money, and, most importantly, it was *'To advocate those views of doctrine and church-order which are most certainly received among us.'* Although he had a certain amount of help in compiling the magazine, and received contributions from various sources, he took personal responsibility for all that went into print, and allowed nothing to be included of which he did not approve. It was very much his own magazine.

He also worked on various Bible commentaries and devotional books. In 1865 he published *Morning by Morning,* a book of daily Bible readings with suitable comments. This was followed by *Evening by Evening,* and in later years he produced *The Cheque Book of the Bank of Faith* – three hundred and thirty six Bible promises for daily use, with his own commentary. His application of the words of the Bible to the sort of problems Christians were likely to experience in everyday life proved highly successful. Many people wrote to say how a particular day's reading had helped them. But the confidence and authority with which he wrote seemed like arrogance and bombast to the more thoughtful and sensitive reader. Spurgeon never revealed the traumas and crises of his own mature Christian life. In view of the Press's interest in him it is not surprising if he shrank from baring his soul. But had he been able to do so, he could have gained the confidence of a whole new group of cultured, intelligent people. As it was, his greatest influence lay among the working classes, untutored or self-educated, who needed teaching that was easy to understand but authoritative in its approach.

In 1866 everything at the Tabernacle was well organised and running smoothly. Spurgeon felt in need of a new challenge, so he encouraged the church to pray for a new work to be sent them. Sure enough, not long afterward a Mrs Hillyard gave Spurgeon twenty thousand pounds with which to found an orphanage. A site was bought at Stockwell, and building commenced. It was decided to build several houses where the children could live as in families, with house-parents. Only boys were catered for at first; girls were not taken until 1880, when four houses were specially built for them. After the College, the Orphanage was nearest Spurgeon's heart. He tried to spend every Christmas Day with the children, and bought presents for all of them. He would enter the big playroom with the boys and laugh delightedly as they scrambled for the coppers he scattered among them.

So the work grew and prospered. By October 1867 the Tabernacle had a membership of three and a half thousand. Spurgeon needed full-time help with the pastoral care, and it was decided to invite his brother James to be Assistant Pastor. James accepted the invitation, and worked during the week in Southwark. He spent his Sundays preaching to a small congregation in Croydon. By now Spurgeon had given up all pastoral visiting. Instead he set aside Tuesday afternoons, when anyone who wished to see him could come to the Tabernacle. Even then, numbers were so great that efficient organisation was needed. Several elders would also be there, and they would talk to everybody, dealing with some cases themselves and giving others a card of introduction to the pastor. Spurgeon interviewed these privately in his vestry; he made a point of speaking to every applicant for baptism or membership. He was a stickler for church discipline, and had no hesitation in refusing anybody whose laxness of conduct threw doubt on the genuineness of their conversation. In later life he said that he had refused 'many people' admission to the Tabernacle.

By the winter of 1869 his health was showing signs of the tremendous demands upon him. He had several attacks of illness, not least of which was a bout of smallpox. Fortunately it was not a virulent strain, and he recovered. However, a much more painful malady struck him in December: it was gout, and he was to suffer from it repeatedly until his death. It affected his hands and feet first, but later it spread, got a hold on his internal organs, and led to Bright's disease and congestion of the lungs. Even in its early stages it was extremely painful, and an attack left him too weak to work. The disease also affected his nervous system and made him prone to depression. It was particualarly bad in the winter time, but was also liable to affect him in mild weather. In the early summer of 1871 he had to cancel a tour he planned to make to the Continent. He did, however, manage to visit Antwerp in August, taking the twins along with him. They were nearly fifteen, and old enough to take an interest in the various museums and churches their father showed them. It was not a dull tour with Spurgeon as their guide. He knew a tremendous amount about architecture and about famous artists and sculptors, and he kept Charles and Thomas enthralled.

Towards the end of 1871 Spurgeon was feeling very depressed. Apart from his gout, he was anxious about his work at the Tabernacle. During 1871 he had been absent for quite long periods – more than ever before. The congregation had been drawn to the Tabernacle by his preaching; would they stay if they had to put up with so many temporary substitutes? The church was sure of its own loyalty to its beloved pastor, and decided to do without him for that winter. They gave him a holiday and he made a tour of Italy, visiting Rome, Naples, Pompeii and the Riviera. It did him a great deal of good. He found in succeeding years that it was essential for him to take regular winter breaks in the mild climate of South Europe.

He had proved his people's loyalty, and need have no anxiety on that score. In fact, he came to have such a tremendous confidence in his flock that it was excessively painful to him to be given a bad report of them. There was one case of gross discourtesy to a temporary minister, when a significant number of the congregation walked out as soon as they realised that Spurgeon would not be taking the service. Spurgeon could not bring himself to believe the story. Not even his love for truth could dispel the illusion that his was a perfect congregation.

When Spurgeon was in good health he found that the best way to relax and refresh himself was to take a trip into the country. He loved trees and plants, and a trip to the New Forest, such as he made in June 1873, was a real treat to him. He bought a ramshackle old carriage and an old horse for these excursions, caring nothing for the disapproval of 'respectable' people. He would invite College students to go along with him, and enjoyed their amazed laughter when they saw him for the first time in this disreputable equipage. He never cared much about appearances. He dressed so casually as to provoke the surprised comment of the society journal *The World*:

> '*Wrapped in a rough blue overcoat, with a species of soft deerstalking hat on his head, a loose black necktie round his massive throat, and a cigar burning merrily in his mouth, he is surely the most unclerical of all the preachers of the Gospel.*'

If he was very busy and could only get away for a couple of hours, he would drive through nearby Addington Park, which belonged to Dr Benson, the Archbishop of Canterbury. Every year Dr Benson sent round a card giving Spurgeon the right of free passage through his park, and more than once he entertained the dissenting preacher to lunch at Addington. The social division between Church and Dissent was so great that even when Spurgeon met leading Anglicans informally, both were conscious of their respective doctrinal positions, and very aware that they were going against custom. Dr Benson knew that his butler, footman and coachman all attended the Tabernacle; he must have had a sharp sense of the incongruity of entertaining his servants' minister. As we have seen in the Baptismal Regeneration controversy, Spurgeon generally respected Anglicans, although he believed they were wrong in their adherence to the Prayer Book. In early 1873 the Tabernacle bought a plot of ground near the Chapel from the Church of England, on which to erect a new building for the Pastor's College. Spurgeon's remark on the occasion, though said in fun, reveals his underlying attitude to the Established Church. He reported that he had *'Secured the parson's garden, behind the Tabernacle, as the site for the new College, and he was going to cultivate it for him by growing dissenters on it!'*

In 1874 Spurgeon had the joy of baptising his eighteen year-old sons at the Tabernacle. Young Charles felt that he was called by God to be a pastor like his father, and the following year he entered Pastor's

College. Thomas showed great artistic promise, and was apprenticed to a wood-engraver. But his health was giving cause for concern; his lungs were 'weak'. Perhaps he began to show signs of tuberculosis. At any rate the doctors recommended a long sea voyage, and in 1877 he set sail for Australia.

By the 1870's Susie's health had deteriorated so that she was a chronic invalid. It was a great sorrow to her that she could not attend the services at the Tabernacle, and was therefore out of touch with much of the work that was going on. In 1875, however, she discovered something that she could do herself, and which brought her into contact (by post) with Christians both at home and abroad. Spurgeon's *Lectures to my Students* had just been published, and Susie wished that she could *'Place it in the hands of every minister in England.'* *'Why not do so? How much will you give?'* challenged her husband. Susie remembered that she had a small hoard of crown pieces that she had been saving; when she looked at it she found she had enough money to buy one hundred copies of the three-volume work. They were soon sent out to various ministers Susie knew would appreciate them. She and Charles knew that clerical salaries were generally rather low, but they were unprepared for the flood of requests for free books that poured in as the Book Fund came to be heard of throughout the country. They read accounts that wrung their hearts of ministers whose charges expected them to dress respectably, buy theological books and assist the poor on a pittance that could not even maintain a single family. Susie eagerly collected donations to her Fund and was able to buy and send out thousands of volumes. Charles dug deep into his own pocket to send financial assistance to the worst cases. He was proud of Susie's involvement in this labour of love, and commented in *The Sword and the Trowel,*

> *'You should see her stores, her book-room, her busy helpers on the parcel-day, and the waggon-load of books each fortnight. The Book Fund at certain hours is the ruling idea of our house. Every day it occupies the head and heart of its manager. The reader has scant idea of the book-keeping involved in the book-giving; but this may be said – the loving manager has more than six thousand names on her lists, and yet she knows every volume that each man has received from the first day until now. The work is not muddled, but done as if by clockwork, yet it is performed with a hearty desire to give pleasure to all receivers, and to trouble no applicant with needless inquiries.'*

The books sent out were mainly Spurgeon's own works. His massive commentary on the Psalms, *The Treasury of David,* was most in demand.

Susie had enough helpers to continue the work even when she herself was too ill to do it. In the summer of 1878 she took a serious turn for the worse, and Thomas was telegraphed to return from Australia. By the time he landed in Plymouth after a lengthy voyage, his mother was much better. But his father fell seriously ill almost at once, and it seemed as if God had caused Thomas to come home in order to be a help and support to the Pastor. For on his Australian trip Thomas had discovered his true calling: he found in himself an ability and a desire to be a preacher like his father. He preached for the first time in the Tabernacle on the tenth of November. Young Charles, by now pastor of a chapel in Greenwich, also took a turn at 'supplying' the pulpit.

By the new year Spurgeon, though crippled with gout, was well enough to travel, and he set off for Menton on the Riviera, taking with him his son Thomas, his valet 'old George' Lovejoy, and his friend and publisher Joseph Passmore. He had been to Menton several times since 1872, and was becoming known in the little resort. French, English and Italians welcomed him with delight. He stayed at the Hotel de la Paix, and gradually improved in health. A Dr Henry Bennet, who lived in Menton, gave Spurgeon permission to use his garden as often as he liked. Spurgeon could usually manage the walk from the hotel to the garden. There were a number of Christians staying or living in Menton, with whom Spurgeon was very glad to have fellowship, ranging in denomination from Anglicans to Mennonite Baptists. George Muller and Hudson Taylor, the one famous for his orphanage, the other for his missionary work, talked often with Spurgeon, and their courage and faith was an inspiration to him.

Sunday services were held in the villa of one of the English residents. The leading Christians took it in turn to preach; even Thomas took a turn. His father, however, was not well enough to do so this year. He was just able to take Thomas' education in hand and begin his preparation for a career as a full-time pastor. Thomas regarded this as a special course of the Pastor's College.

Spurgeon returned to London in April, anxious to take up his duties even though his friends doubted whether he was really well enough. Spurgeon liked anniversaries and birthdays, and could look forward to the celebration of his pastoral silver jubilee in May. He had served the chapel for twenty-five years, and the congregation was bent on making it an occasion for celebration. The event lasted for three days, culminating in a tea at the Tabernacle and a special meeting for prayer and praise. The congregation (and Spurgeon) had plenty to praise God for: during the twenty-five years of his pastorate nine thousand people had joined the church. Of course, not even the Tabernacle could contain this number; Spurgeon encouraged large groups to leave and to establish daughter chapels in the region of South London. In this way the influence of the Tabernacle was spreading ever further.

In 1880 the Spurgeons moved to 'Westwood', a fine house set in extensive grounds in Upper Norwood. They hoped that the more rural atmosphere and higher ground would be better for their health. But as far as Charles was concerned, the only thing that would cure him was a complete cessation of work – and he would never consent to that.

Soon after they were settled at Westwood the house

was burgled. The only item of value taken was a gold-headed stick which had been given by a friend. The thief hammered the gold out of shape, then tried to sell the stick at a pawnbroker's in Southwark. However, he had failed to obliterate Spurgeon's name, and so the police were alerted. But their man escaped. The incident got into the papers, and consequently Spurgeon received a letter which he always believed came from 'his' thief. In effect he apologised for burgling *'the horflings' Spurgin'*, ('the orphans' Spurgeon') and suggested he keep a dog. So Punch was introduced into the household – a pug dog of whom Spurgeon said that *'he knew more than any dog ever ought to know.'*

With the money gained from the sale of the misshapen gold Spurgeon was able to buy several books, which were more use to him, he reckoned, than the stick could have been – particularly as he did not walk much at all now his gout was so troublesome. He constantly bought books, and by the time he died he left more than twelve thousand volumes. He gave away many more, to the Pastor's College library and to individual students – not to mention those that he lent and did not receive back! In Westwood the books filled the study and the library, a smaller room off the study (the 'den') and a vestibule outside the study. He possessed hundreds of commentaries on the Bible as well as all sorts of other devotional and theological works. He also had biographies, books of travel and adventure, and whole shelves full of books on natural history and science. He was not nearly so interested in fiction or poetry. There was, of course, a complete set of his own books and a large but incomplete collection of reprints and translations of his sermons.

He made a hobby of collecting autographs and photographs of as many authors as he could. Those of Ruskin and Dr Livingstone had pride of place. He was pleased to have copies of books annotated in the margin by their former owners, especially if they were well-known individuals. He himself scribbled comments in his books. In F. D. Maurice's *Prophets and Kings of the Old Testament* he wrote, '*Herein we find a great deal of wild doctrine, but yet there is thought of no mean order. We can wash out the gold.*' Dr Pusey on *The Minor Prophets* is '*Invaluable*'. Spurgeon could appreciate the scholarly achievements of those with whom he disagreed on theological grounds.

Spurgeon drew on his extensive knowledge of theological books when he came to write his review of commentaries, *Commenting and Commentaries*. Although most of the commentaries he recommended are now out of date, it is still interesting to see what he thought of the books that were available in his day. Naturally, Calvin's commentaries were given a high recommendation.

Spurgeon's silver wedding anniversary was celebrated at Westwood in February 1881. He had been too ill to keep the actual date, the eighth of January. Charles and Susie's way of celebrating was to invite the deacons to hold their regular Deacon's Meeting at Westwood instead of at the Tabernacle. The usual business would be followed by a celebration tea. It is a mark of Spurgeon's close involvement with the church that he regarded all his deacons as personal friends, and that he felt he could combine church-business with such an intimate celebration.

Only a few years later Spurgeon had another anniversary to celebrate, that of his fiftieth birthday on the nineteenth of June 1884. He had, as usual, been ill during the winter months. A spell in Menton had restored him, but he fell ill again on his return to the Tabernacle in February. During his confinement at Westwood the church enthusiastically passed this resolution:

> *'That the church gratefully recognises the goodness of Almighty God in sparing to it, and to the Church at large, the invaluable life of our beloved Pastor, C.H. Spurgeon; and that, in order worthily to celebrate his Jubilee, a suitable memorial be raised, and presented to him; and that it be an instruction to the deacons to take this matter vigorously in hand, and to carry it forward as they may deem best.'*

The church was determined to give some gift to Spurgeon in return for all that he had done for them; they hoped that he could be persuaded to accept a testimonial for his own benefit. He usually gave away any money that he received.

The date of the Jubilee celebrations became widely known through the press, and many people sent letters of congratulation, or came in person to shake him by the hand and make a contribution to the testimonial fund. Spurgeon spent five hours in his vestry in the Tabernacle, receiving all these well-wishers. A celebration tea was laid on, followed by a meeting in the Tabernacle for all those connected with the work of the chapel. D. L. Moody, the American evangelist, was present and spoke of what Spurgeon's sermons had meant to him. To Spurgeon's joy Susie was well enough to be present at the celebrations; but her own delight was marred by the knowledge that the Fenians (supporters of Irish Home Rule) had threatened to blow up the Tabernacle. Besides Susie, only a few Tabernacle officials knew of this; the police had decided to keep it secret and let the Jubilee take its course. Spurgeon was not told. He might have decided he could not risk the lives of all his people for the sake of his celebrations. So the only difference at the Tabernacle was the presence of a large number of uniformed and plain-clothes policemen. The secret had to be kept for another day. A public meeting was arranged for the following evening at which many prominent people, including the Earl of Shaftesbury, spoke of the good that had been done by Spurgeon and his church. The testimonial was presented to Spurgeon in the form of a cheque for forty-five hundred pounds. He declared he would use most of it to support the various projects of the Tabernacle; he might keep a small amount for his own use.

Only after all the hullabaloo was over, and they were in their carriage driving home, could Susie tell

Charles of the awful threat that had hung over them. Then and there they thanked God for his loving care of them. The police were not absolutely sure that the danger was past, and for a while afterwards kept a careful watch on the Tabernacle.

Many comments were made at this time about Spurgeon's position in the theological world. He was well established by now, a far more respectable figure than in the early days when the press had jeered and sniped at him. He had done a tremendous amount towards changing the religious climate of the period, introducing a new naturalness and realism in pulpit manners. Other churches had begun to emulate him, particularly in a concern to communicate with the working classes. The British Church was rapidly becoming 'Spurgeonised'.

Spurgeon himself, however, was of the opinion that there was still in the religious world a good deal of disagreement with his theological position, if not downright opposition. In an interview with W.T. Stead, printed for his Jubilee in the *Pall Mall Gazette*, he said,

> *'In theology I stand where I did when I began preaching, and I stand almost alone. If I ever did such a thing, I could preach my earliest sermons now without change so far as the essential doctrines are concerned. I stand almost exactly where Calvin stood in his maturer years; not where he stood in his* Institutes, *which he wrote when quite a young man*

but in his later works; that position is taken by few.
Even those who occupy Baptist pulpits do not
preach exactly the same truths I preach.'

Such a statement is rather puzzling, for Spurgeon
knew as well as anyone that Calvin developed and
rewrote his *Institutes* as he grew older, and that the
definitive edition – the one published by the Calvin
Translation Society, which he himself recommended
in *Commenting and Commentaries* – was published
originally in 1559-1560, only four years before its
author's death. Certainly Spurgeon had a deep understanding of the Reformer's theology, and taught
aspects of it that were perhaps misunderstood by
even the hyper-Calvinists. For example, the hyper-
Calvinists believed that Christ's Atonement was
limited because he only died for the elect. Spurgeon
held, with Calvin, that Christ died for all, but that he
does not pray for all; it is his prayer, his intercession
before the Father's throne, that ensures the election of
any individual.

Spurgeon was thinking of theological issues, but he
was also perhaps feeling more in sympathy with the
controversial aspect of Calvin's later writings. In his
final edition of the *Institutes* the Reformer was at such
pains to meet all objections that, as the modern scholar
François Wendel says,

'Much more than in the earlier editions he subjects
his adversaries to the most varied and unseemly

abuse, which detracts from the rest of an exposition
that is so judicious and intended to be scientific.'

In the Baptismal Regeneration controversy Spurgeon
had already upset fellow-Christians by what seemed to
them an uncharitable emphasis on the unscriptural
basis for the position which they adopted in all good
conscience. In his old age, it seems, he was becoming
less tolerant of other Christian bodies, and more fun-
damentalist in his outlook. He was already, in his
fiftieth year, feeling isolated from his own denomination, and seeing himself as the only upholder of Christian truth. This feeling was to grow stronger and
stronger until it resulted, in his final years of life, in
the Down-grade Controversy.

It seemed to Spurgeon that in the 1880's the stan-
dard of the Faith was slipping. Scepticism was ram-
pant, and many found it impossible to believe in the
miraculous element contained in the Bible. What
troubled Spurgeon most was that many Christian
ministers seemed to be affected by this malady of
unbelief. The Congregational Church appeared to be
in serious trouble. In 1874 R.W. Dale (with whom
Spurgeon had previously been on cordial terms) stated
his disbelief in eternal punishment. He did not go so
far as to adopt the idea of universal salvation, but
supposed that the wicked are simply annihilated at
death. At the session of the Congregational Union in
1887 its chairman, Alexander MacKennal, said that
Congregationalists rejected dogma — finalised state-

ments about the nature of God and the world – but retained doctrine – a progressing understanding of the same. One of the dogmas the Congregationalists rejected was that of the literal inspiration and inerrancy of the Bible.

In Spurgeon's eyes the trouble lay in an acceptance of Higher Criticism as a valid method of interpreting the Bible. It treated the Bible as if it were an ordinary historical document and brought the same critical methods to bear on it. Spurgeon saw this as a readiness to pursue the wisdom of men rather than that of God. He wrote an article for *The Sword and the Trowel* in which he complained that the Faith was being downgraded:

> *'Attendance at places of worship is declining and reverence for holy things is vanishing; and we solemnly believe this to be largely attributable to the scepticism which has flashed from the pulpit and spread among the people.'*

Only by treating the Bible as the infallible word of God could the old faith be restored. Meanwhile there was the question of church discipline;

> *'It now becomes a serious question how far those who abide by the faith once delivered to the saints should fraternize with those who have turned aside to another gospel.'*

Spurgeon knew that the rot was spreading in the Baptist Union also, and he hoped that the issue would be debated at its forthcoming session; but the conference, held in Sheffield in the autumn of 1887, passed by without any reference to what had already become known as 'the Down-Grade Question'. Spurgeon resigned from the Union.

Such a step might have been accepted without comment by the Baptist Union, although they could ill afford to lose their most important and influential member. But in the November Spurgeon took the matter a step further by including an article in *The Sword and the Trowel* in which he accused the Baptists of tolerating sin, and of therefore being in sin themselves. They preferred denominational peace and fellowship to the upset that would ensue if they began to purge themselves. *'But,'* Spurgeon warned, *'it is our solemn conviction that where there can be no real spiritual communion there should be no pretence of fellowship.* Fellowship with known and vital error is participation in sin.'

By this time he was once again in the South of France, and had to deal with the Baptist Union by correspondence. The matter was complicated by misunderstandings and consequent ill-will which arose between Spurgeon and the leaders of the Baptist Union. In the eyes of the Union Spurgeon had left precipitately, without taking the proper steps to see that the issue was dealt with by the Baptist Council. Spurgeon felt that was merely an excuse, for he had written and spoken about the Down-Grade issue, albeit informally, to both the Secretary and the President. However, he was still willing to meet the representatives of the Union to discuss the matter, and did so on his return to London in January 1888. He proposed, for the maintenance of doctrinal unity, that an evangelical Declaration of Faith should be adopted, to which all members of the Union must subscribe. For the hundreds of years Baptist Churches had been in existence the only formal bond between them had been the acceptance of the principle of adult baptism by total immersion.

The Council drew up a Declaration of Faith, intending to bring it before the Assembly of the Union the following April. They showed it to Spurgeon, but he was suspicious of it. He felt it had been drawn up in a spirit of compromise, that it was too ambiguous. He wanted a document that could not be misunderstood or misinterpreted, and which would have the effect of excluding any laxness of doctrine. Nevertheless it was presented to the Assembly. The effect of Spurgeon's opposition, though not all the members realised this, was that a vote for the Declaration would be a vote of censure on Spurgeon. The Assembly voted overwhelmingly for the Declaration; only seven took Spurgeon's side. Spurgeon was convinced now that he had been right in resigning.

The narrowness of his outlook had blinded him to what the 'Down-Graders' were trying to do. It was not so much Higher Criticism that was at fault as the prevailing spirit of the age. Disbelief in the supernatural reached its height in the 1880's, and many ministers of the Gospel found it an impossible task to preach Christianity on the basis of signs and wonders. Instead they tried to bring people to a deeper faith, a faith which rested on the person of Christ alone, and was not bolstered up by a dependence on miracles. Spurgeon's condemnation seemed to them to show not only a lack of love, but also an unwillingness to understand the problems involved. His ministry was largely to simple, uneducated people who were as yet untouched by the prevailing materialism. The Gospel as the Puritans had written about it and understood it still had an appeal to them. But to an increasing number of people the language and thought-forms of the Puritans was becoming unintelligible. Spurgeon accused his fellow-ministers of preaching 'another gospel', but it was more a question of presentation than of content. Spurgeon's wish for a comprehensive doctrinal formula could never be fulfilled. How could he ever have expected mere words to contain the mysteries of Incarnation and Atonement without possibility of misunderstanding? The Baptists preferred to rest their faith on the unseen but Living Word; Spurgeon was relying too much on the rigidity of phrases and formulae.

Spurgeon blamed the Down-Grade controversy, and not overwork, for the illness leading to his early death. After the Baptist Assembly of 1888 his health became progressively worse. The gout was affecting his lungs, and his kidneys were beginning to fail — he had Bright's disease. He continued to go to Menton every winter, staying now at the Hotel Beau Rivage.

He drove himself hard even here, writing for *The Sword and the Trowel,* dealing with correspondence, and working on theological books. In these last few years he was preparing a commentary on Matthew, *The Gospel of the Kingdom,* which he left unfinished. He was also writing notes for his autobiography. He continued to preach at the Tabernacle in the summer, but found it an increasing trial. In April 1891 he found himself in a *'Low, nervous condition'* in the pulpit, and had much ado to get through the service. He preached his last sermon on the seventh of June. In October A.T. Pierson, an American Presbyterian minister, was appointed as temporary minister to the Tabernacle and Spurgeon set out for Menton. To his great satisfaction Susie was well enough to accompany him. His brother James came with his wife, and his private secretary Joseph Harrald completed the party.

By the new year Spurgeon's health had improved enough for him to conduct a few services in his hotel suite. On the seventeenth of January he gave out as the final hymn for the evening service one that was most appropriate for what turned out to be his own last hymn. The words are by Samuel Rutherford, one of his beloved Puritans:

'The sands of time are sinking,
The dawn of heaven breaks,
The summer morn I've sighed for,
The fair, sweet morn awakes.
Dark, dark has been the midnight
But dayspring is at hand,

For glory, glory dwelleth
In Immanuel's land.'

Three days later he had a relapse, and had to go to bed. The following Tuesday (twenty-sixth) he was only partly conscious. By a strange irony that was the day the Tabernacle had chosen for a service of thanksgiving for the improvement in his health. Spurgeon roused himself enough to order a hundred pounds to be sent from himself and Susie towards the Tabernacle expenses. Then he lost consciousness, and remained insensible until his death on the last day of January. His body was brought to London. Memorial and funeral services were held at the Tabernacle for five days from February the seventh, with at least a hundred thousand people attending. He was buried in Norwood cemetery.

At the end of his long pastorate the church had five thousand three hundred and eleven members, while over the years fourteen thousand six hundred and ninety one had been received into fellowship. His achievement was on a colossal scale. The work did not cease on his death, but continued with his son Thomas as Pastor. Young Charles took over the Orphanage. The Tabernacle was largely destroyed by fire in October 1898. With typical enthusiasm and resourcefulness the congregation rebuilt it. Susie died in 1903, and two years later Westwood was sold. The library went to William Jewell College, Missouri, where it is to this day.

Spurgeon should be remembered not for his later

years, clouded as they were by bitter controversy and failing health, but for his vigorous middle years, when he was loved by his church and respected by the Christian world at large. His work in organising the efficient running of his gigantic church was an achievement in itself, but it is as a preacher that he made his most significant contribution to the cause of Christianity. Through his sermons, both spoken and printed, many thousands have been led to their all-important encounter with Christ.

BIBLIOGRAPHY

Bacon E.W.   *Spurgeon, Heir to the Puritans*
                 (George Allen & Unwin, 1967)

Chadwick, O.   *The Victorian Church*
                 (A & C Black, 1966)

Kendall, R.T.   *Calvin and English Calvinism to 1649*
                 (Oxford University Press, 1979)

Murray, I.   *The Forgotten Spurgeon* (Banner of
                 Truth Trust, 1973)

Pike, G.H.   *The Life and Work of Charles
                 Haddon Spurgeon*
                 (Cassell & Co. 1984)

Spurgeon, C.H.   *The Early Years*   (condensed from
                 1962   C H Spurgeon's
                 The Full Harvest   *Autobiography,*
                 1973   4 vols, 1897-1900)

                 (Banner of Truth Trust)

                 Lectures to My Students
                 (Passmore & Alabaster, 1876)

Wendel, F.   *Calvin* (Fontana, 1965).